YOUR KNOWLEDGE HAS VALUE

Simon Etzel

The MBA - is it worth it?

GRIN Verlag

Bibliografische Information der Deutschen Nationalbibliothek:

Die Deutsche Bibliothek verzeichnet diese Publikation in der Deutschen National-
bibliografie; detaillierte bibliografische Daten sind im Internet über http://dnb.d-
nb.de/ abrufbar.

Imprint:

Copyright © 2013 GRIN Verlag GmbH
Druck und Bindung: Books on Demand GmbH, Norderstedt Germany
ISBN: 978-3-656-64573-3

This book at GRIN:

http://www.grin.com/en/e-book/272573/the-mba-is-it-worth-it

GRIN - Your knowledge has value

Der GRIN Verlag publiziert seit 1998 wissenschaftliche Arbeiten von Studenten, Hochschullehrern und anderen Akademikern als eBook und gedrucktes Buch. Die Verlagswebsite www.grin.com ist die ideale Plattform zur Veröffentlichung von Hausarbeiten, Abschlussarbeiten, wissenschaftlichen Aufsätzen, Dissertationen und Fachbüchern.

Visit us on the internet:

http://www.grin.com/

http://www.facebook.com/grincom

http://www.twitter.com/grin_com

University of Applied Sciences Stuttgart
Field of study: Business Management
Study course: General Management

Hochschule
für Technik
Stuttgart

The MBA – is it worth it?

Table of contents

List of Abbreviations

GMAT   -   Graduate Management Admission Test

MBA   -   Master of Business Administration

SWOT   -   Strengths, Weaknesses, Opportunities and Threats

1 Introduction

The question of whether the MBA is worth it or not has caused much debate over the last years. As far back as the nineties, a discussion about the value of the MBA is held. In those days, a strong decrease in the number of applicants at American business schools was proof enough for the decline of the MBA in general (Celis, 1993). Today's reality is that there are 12,000 business schools in the world and the demand remained unbroken (Entrepreneur, 2012). In America, even a persistent shortage of talented mid-level leaders is the case for two-third of all businesses.

Despite of an MBA title or not, business skills should be accessible to a lot more people preparing them for the next economic crises. The trend in many industrial countries is that the so-called baby boomers are retiring and not enough young business leaders are to follow. Therefore, efficiency enhancements, allocating resources and eventually getting good results will be even more important. According to Hay Group, a global management consulting firm, "organizations will have to radically adapt their cultures, structures, systems and processes in order to survive the new world order" (Tauber, 2013). For that reason, business specialists are essential. There is some controversy as to whether they need to have an MBA degree or not.

2 The MBA – What Exactly Is It?

The Master of Business Administration, better known as MBA, is "an **advanced college degree**, earned by those who successfully graduate from their college or university's MBA program. As it is the case with other advanced degrees, traditionally a student will have already received a Bachelors degree in some area of study, before working towards his or her MBA" (BusinessDictionary.com, 2013). The MBA is presently the most popular professional degree program in the world. By now there are over 2,500 different MBA programs offered **worldwide**. The first of them were introduced at American universities around the turn of the 20th century (Find-mba.com, n.d.).

A first distinction is made between a general MBA, which is usually shorter in duration, and a specialized MBA, which may take longer. Latter with the addition that one is already positioned in a particular departmental function and therefore might be more marketable in the end. There are several **core topics** MBA programs are dedicated to, including:

- Accounting
- Business strategy
- Economics
- Finance
- Human resources/organization management
- Marketing
- Manufacturing/production
- Operations
- Statistics/quantitative methods
- Technology/information systems (Hansen, n.d.).

MBA programs are structured around these core courses, typically taken at the beginning, and are supplemented by elective courses which allow further specializations. Generally, all courses can be divided into analytical, functional and specialization (Mba.com, n.d.).

There are several **types of MBA programs** in the international education market. Students are able to complete their advanced degree, amongst others, in a regular "Two-Year Full-Time MBA program", an accelerated "One-Year Full-Time program", part-time, "Executive MBA programs" – where participants work full-time and normally have a higher level of working experience and "Distance Learning programs" – where classes are held off-campus (Mba.com, n.d.).

People willing to participate in a MBA program usually have to fulfill a set of ambitious **admission criteria**. Those criteria is usually made up of a combination of the Graduate Management Admission Test (GMAT) - "a computer adaptive test which assesses a person's analytical, writing, quantitative, verbal, and reading skills in standard written English" – motivational letters, essays, academic transcripts and work experience. Sometimes, also extracurricular activities are taken into consideration (Mba.com, n.d.).

3 Is It Worth Doing an MBA?

It is not surprising that the answers to this question vary significantly depending on who is being asked. On the one hand, experts take the view that especially in present times of financial crises an MBA is a ticket gaining entry into popular companies, senior managing positions and high salaries. Surveys have proven that not only the MBA degree itself but also the school one has chosen is a criterion for business leaders to select one job candidate over another. Leading to the result that graduates from business schools with a good reputation are not at risk of becoming unemployed (Schuetze, 2011). Another point putting forth the opinion that the MBA is valuable is that companies which are anxious to compete successfully in a globalized world need business specialists in order to be sustainable and thriving. According to data gathered by IBM, a worldwide operating information technology giant, and others, the main reasons why businesses fail are simple. They do not understand and therefore define the customer needs properly, face insufficient resources and have indefinite business strategies. Exactly these kinds of problems MBA students learn to deal with during their business education (Tauber, 2013).

On the other hand, specialists state that something is broken in the world of management education. MBA graduates are to blame for the recent economic meltdowns and they are focused on earning instead of learning. On top of that, current teaching methods do not produce managers but rather people full of hubris unwilling and unable to change (Bradshaw, 2009). Another argument often put forward doubts whether the investment in an MBA is worth the money, estimated about $150,000 in the U.S. (Stephens, 2013). It is also said that MBA students will often learn the same things they already know from their undergraduate degree, especially when it comes to general MBA programs, and the new skills they pick up from an MBA could be limited (Robin, 2013).

In order to get a clearer overview about the pros and cons of an MBA the following chapter starts with the approach of a SWOT analysis.

3.1 MBA SWOT Analysis

The SWOT analysis is a strategic planning method and is used to evaluate the **S**trengths, **W**eaknesses, **O**pportunities and **T**hreats involved in a business venture. In this case, it helps to form an opinion whether an MBA is useful or not.

Strengths
First, one gets general knowledge across multiple business topics. Second, an MBA program teaches a variety of tools helping to make proper analyses and eventually decisions. Third, an MBA degree stands out on ones resume and has proven to be attractive for business leaders. Fourth, it boosts the earning power the minute a master student graduates.

Weaknesses
Although MBA programs offer a diversified business education one is still not an expert in anything. This may be especially the case for general programs. The previously mentioned tools are hardly ever used in work life. On-the-job experience might be more important than theoretical knowledge. It is difficult to identify in advance if the investment for an MBA is worth it. Among other things, tuition fees, living expenses and opportunity costs have to be taken into consideration. The last weakness is on an inter-personal level: co-workers might feel inferior which could lead to tension within work groups, departments and beyond.

Opportunities
A closer look at numerous studies indicates that an MBA helps people to make progress in their careers. But not only a progress in the career path pursued before attending business school again is possible, it will also help to make a career change and to explore new avenues. Chances are good

that graduates are building an extensive network during their student days, which is essential in professional lives nowadays.

Threats

Even though an MBA degree enables people to attain senior management positions it is quite common to start from the lower ranks anyway. Furthermore, the MBA is a door opener in the first place. After that the career progression is, in most cases, purely based on the performance on the job. This is aggravated by the fact that students graduating during an economic downturn would be lucky to get back their old jobs (Karampela, 2013).

Turning now to the question if an MBA is worth it and focusing this specific issue more precisely in the following chapter.

3.2 Reasons Why the MBA Is Worthwhile

One point is that the MBA is one of the most helpful tools a businessperson can have. It not only gives an advantage in the global labor market, but it also teaches adaptability in a modern economy in which career-switching and on-going change are the norm. Another argument is that students have the possibility to create a social network, which might turn out to be very valuable for a future work life. It can also be said that it is simply inefficient to learn things by experience or by one's own initiative when there are formal courses providing the necessary knowledge (Entrepreneur, 2012).

There is growing evidence that having an MBA degree leverages its owners in new job titles and higher salaries. Especially when it comes to reaching senior management positions this title is still important. According to a salary guide, the possible wage increase ranges between $10,000 and $30,000 a year compared to a bachelor's degree. It might also give an advantage in achieving a better work-life balance due to fewer working hours in some cases (Hansen, n.d.).

The Boston Consulting Group develops the claim that business is getting more complex. They state that the global economy has become hyper-competitive; by 2020 up to 60% will do business in foreign markets. Volatility in both revenues and profit margins have tripled in the last 50 years and disruptions to competitive positions are occurring twice as often as in the past. These developments strengthen the need of an MBA. As a result, solid leadership and management are, were and will be essential. Scarce resources need to be allocated efficiently; lasting customer relationships as well as cohesive teams have to be established. Skills, which are taught and developed during a formal business education, called MBA (Tauber, 2013).

Another merit of an MBA program is that students are able to benefit from each other's meaningful work experience since most of the participants have been working and come in with different backgrounds (Entrepreneur, 2012). Benefits are not only received from other students, but also from the business school itself. It is common that those schools maintain strong relationships with companies making it easier for graduates to know where to apply. One example here is the Rotterdam Business School, having special relations to Philips and Unilever, which are headquartered in Amsterdam and Rotterdam. These relationships help both sides: Students know where to apply and increase the chances of becoming an employee. Companies are aware of well-suited graduates (Schuetze, 2011).

In the pages that follow, it is argued why the MBA is not worth it.

3.3 Reasons why the MBA is Pointless

Much of the current debate revolves around an MBA's worth. Critics argue that the degree has lost touch with the real business world. According to them, too much importance is attached to research instead of practical applications. There is no equal balance between theory and practice. Furthermore, they claim that MBA programs failed to develop leaders who are able to cope with a globalized world. Analysts even think that MBA graduates are to blame for the financial crisis because they are focused on profit and share value only, rather than on sustainability and morality. "Conventional MBA programs train the wrong people in the wrong ways with the wrong consequences" (Entrepreneur, 2012).

Let us add to this another observation, which is about the necessary investment in case someone wants to get an MBA degree. Estimations of the costs vary between $100,000 and $180,000 depending on many factors, such as the chosen school. This leads to the argument that if this amount is saved and spent on individual measures the outcome is much higher. Granted that the two core values of an MBA are educational content and a network. The content can be acquired for free using online classes like OpenCourseWare. The remainder could then be used to build a network, by moving on the ground, building relationships with important people and gaining their trust. On top of that, the salary outcome of a 10-week training course in programming for example, which costs about $12,000, results in an average starting salary of $79,000. Whereas the average starting salary for MBA graduates, with little work experience, was $46,630 in 2012 in the US (Stephens, 2013).

Aside from that, having an MBA title does not guarantee that the persons are able to apply what they have learned to the real world. In addition, experts indicate that lifelong learning, keeping and acquiring the required skills and knowledge are, amongst others, the key factors of success (Andersen, 2013).

4 Conclusion

Returning to the question posed at the beginning of this paper, it is now possible to state that there are sufficient grounds for either working towards an MBA or for skipping it.

It is incontestable that MBA aspirants should be clearly aware of the risks and merits MBA studies can mean for them. Moreover, applicants have to know very clearly, why they are doing it and what they want to learn. Answering this question provides knowledge helping to decide which post-graduate qualification might be most useful and which is the right business school (Robin, 2013).

"Consumer behavior, multicultural teams, global markets, political risk and ethical dilemmas" (Tauber, 2013) are complicated and unpredictable. In addition, the challenges of global competitiveness will not be less. Solutions might not fit into textbooks or case studies but suggest that business learning is an ongoing activity. An MBA might be the answer mastering these difficulties. Alternatively, relentless aspiration, endless curiosity and neutral self-awareness might be the vitally needed traits. Maintaining a reasonable balance between initial ineptness and the ability to get through, to lifelong learning and to become a "master of mastery" (Andersen, 2013).

List of Miscellaneous References

Websites

Andersen, Erika, 2013. Why Spending $150K On An MBA is Probably A Dumb Idea [Online]
Available at: http://www.forbes.com/sites/erikaandersen/2013/07/27/why-spending-150k-on-an-mba-is-probably-a-dumb-idea/
[Accessed 13 November 2013].

BusinessDictionary.com, 2013. Masters of Business Administration (MBA). [Online]
Available at: http://www.businessdictionary.com/definition/Masters-of-Business-Administration-MBA.html [Accessed 09 November 2013].

Entrepreneur, 2012. Is an MBA Still Necessary? [Online]
Available at: http://www.entrepreneur.com/article/224440
[Accessed 13 November 2013].

Find-mba.com, n.d. What is an MBA? [Online]
Available at: http://www.find-mba.com/what-is-an-mba [Accessed 10 November 2013].

Karampela, Korina, 2013. Is It Worth Doing an MBA? Part I. [Online]
Available at: http://www.huffingtonpost.co.uk/korina-karampela/is-it-worth-doing-an-mba-_b_2714831.html
[Accessed 10 November 2013].

Mba.com, n.d. Graduate business coursework may look similar from program to program, but no two programs are exactly alike. [Online]
Available at: http://www.mba.com/schools-and-programs/evaluating-schools/curriculum-and-course-selection.aspx [Accessed 09 November 2013].

Mba.com, n.d. What Is a Graduate Business Degree? [Online]
Available at: http://www.mba.com/why-b-school/what-is-a-graduate-business-degree.aspx [Accessed 09 November 2013].

Randall S. Hansen, PH. D., n.d. The Master of Business Administration: Is the MBA Worth the Time, Effort, and Cost?. [Online]
Available at: http://www.quintcareers.com/MBA_degree.html [Accessed 09 November 2013].

Robin, Myriam, 2013. When an MBA isn't worth it: How to tell what degree is best for you. [Online]
Available at: http://leadingcompany.smartcompany.com.au/personal-development/when-an-mba-isnt-worth-it-how-to-tell-what-degree-is-best-for-you/201305224290
[Accessed 10 November 2013].

Stephens, Dale, 2013. A Smart Investor Would Skip the M.B.A.. [Online]
Available at:
http://online.wsj.com/news/articles/SB10001424127887323884304578328243334068564
[Accessed 10 November 2013].

Tauber, Todd, 2013. If MBAs are useless, we're all in big trouble. [Online]
Available at: http://qz.com/79042/if-mbas-are-obsolete-were-all-in-big-trouble/
[Accessed 10 November 2013].

Online Newspaper Articles

Bradshaw, Della, 2009. Deans fight crisis fires with MBA overhaul. Financial
times [internet] 08 June.
Available at: http://www.ft.com/intl/cms/s/0/a2353870-53c4-11de-be08-00144feabdc0.html#axzz2hQUvP4MR
[Accessed 10 November 2013].

Celis, William, 1993. Business Schools Hit Hard Times Amid Doubt Over
Value of M.B.A. New York Times [internet] 12 May.
Available at: http://www.nytimes.com/1993/05/12/education/business-schools-hit-hard-times-amid-doubt-over-value-of-mba.html?pagewanted=all&src=pm
[Accessed 13 November 2013].

Schuetze, Christopher F., 2011. Gauging the Value of Your M.B.A.. New
York Times [internet] 19 October.
Available at: http://www.nytimes.com/2011/10/20/education/20iht-SReducEmploy20.html?pagewanted=all&_r=1&
[Accessed 10 November 2013].